Raising Kids with a

Faith that Lasts

PARTICIPANT'S GUIDE

TYNDALE HOUSE PUBLISHERS, INC.
Carol Stream, Illinois

CONTENTS

QUICK START GUIDE FOR PARENTS

Whether you're studying in a group, as a couple, or individually, this book is for you. It's packed with discussion questions, advice, biblical input, and application activities.

But maybe all you'd like to do right now is watch the accompanying DVD and talk about it with your spouse—or think about it on your own. If so, go directly to the "Catching the Vision" section of each chapter. There you'll find the discussion questions you're looking for.

When you have more time, we encourage you to explore the other features in this book. We think you'll find them . . . essential!

WELCOME!

If there's anything you don't need, it's one more thing to do.

Unless, of course, that one thing might make the *other* things a whole lot easier.

We can't guarantee that this course will take all the challenge out of parenthood. It won't keep your kids from forgetting their lunch money, make them trade in their video games for art museum passes, or remind them to scoop the cat's litter box.

But it *will* help you understand why your parenting is so crucial, how to connect with your kids and encourage them to connect with their Creator, and how to enjoy the journey to the fullest. That's because you'll learn the essentials—what's vital to a healthy parent-child relationship, keys to protecting and training and affirming kids, and what God considers most important in bringing up boys and girls.

In other words, you'll discover how to be the mom or dad you really want to be.

That takes effort, but it doesn't take boredom or busywork. So we've designed this course to be provocative and practical. At its heart is an entertaining, down-to-earth video series featuring many of today's most popular parenting experts. And in your hands is the book that's going to make it all personal for you—the Participant's Guide.

In each chapter of this book, you'll find the following sections:

Finding Yourself. Take this survey to figure out where you stand on the subject at hand.

Catching the Vision. Use this section as you watch and think about the DVD.

Digging Deeper. This Bible study includes Scripture passages and thought-provoking questions.

Making It Work. Practice makes perfect, so here's your chance to begin applying principles from the DVD to your own family.

Bringing It Home. To wrap up, you'll find specific, encouraging advice you can use this week.

Whether you're using this book as part of a group or on your own, taking a few minutes to read and complete each chapter will bring the messages of the DVD home.

And isn't that exactly where you need it most?

Note: Many issues addressed in this series are difficult ones. Some parents may need to address them in greater detail and depth. The DVD presentations and this guide are intended as general advice only, and not to replace clinical counseling, medical treatment, legal counsel, or pastoral guidance.

Focus on the Family maintains a referral network of Christian counselors. For information, call 1-800-A-FAMILY and ask for the counseling department. You can also find plenty of parenting advice and encouragement at www.focusonthefamily.com.

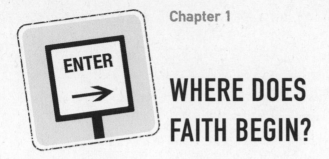

Chapter 1

WHERE DOES FAITH BEGIN?

I've watched the growing popularity of a terrible, almost cowardly philosophy. It says something like, "Well, I wouldn't want to unduly influence my children with my beliefs. They ought to develop their own faith. So I won't try to tell them what I believe. I don't want to ram it down their throats. If they look closely, they'll pick up what I believe just by watching me. Otherwise, I want them to find their own way."

Said in the right tone of voice, those statements almost sound wise. But a parent who thinks that way is actually betraying his or her kids. It's like saying, "I'll teach my child how to tie his shoes and brush his teeth, but I won't teach him about God. That's too important. He can figure that out on his own."

The more important something is, the more we need to make sure our kids understand it. We don't teach them how to walk, then let them discover how to cross a busy highway on their own without any directions or warnings!

What can be more important than what we believe about right and wrong? If we've found the reality of God's love and grace in our lives, how can we not desire the same for our children?

—Carey Casey

CEO, National Center for Fathering[1]

Identifying Your Needs

Here's a questionnaire to get you thinking about how you relate to the subject of spiritual training.

1. When you were a child, who was the closest thing you had to a spiritual mentor?
   ____ your mother
   ____ your father
   ____ Dick Clark on *American Bandstand*
   ____ other _____

2. What part of your early spiritual journey would you like your child to experience, too?
   ____ warm fellowship around the campfire
   ____ a missions trip
   ____ being terrified by midnight showings of movies about the end times
   ____ other _____

3. When it comes to spiritually mentoring your child, what have you tried so far?
   ____ nothing
   ____ memorizing books of the Bible that start with "Q"
   ____ showing how to multiply loaves and fishes
   ____ other _____

4. What's your biggest fear about spiritually training your child?
   ____ that you've waited too long to start
   ____ that she'll reject your attempts to guide her

___ that he'll turn into a spiritual giant and you won't be able to find shoes the right size

___ other _____

5. If spiritually training a child is like passing a baton in a relay race, then

___ you've already dropped the baton.

___ your child doesn't want the baton.

___ you'd rather try the javelin throw.

___ other _____

6. By the time you're done with this study, you hope to

___ see spiritual progress in your child.

___ feel more confident in guiding your child's spiritual growth.

___ learn how to work the remote on your DVD player.

___ other _____

CATCHING THE VISION

Watching and Discussing the DVD

In this DVD segment, author and pastor Mark Holmen challenges parents to pass the baton of faith to their kids. That, he says, is the way to keep from losing so many young adults who were raised in Christian families.

According to Mark, the enemy wants to break the church for years to come by getting Christ and Christlike living out of the home. It's a strategy that's made progress—since many of us would have to search three or four generations back to find ancestors who prayed, read the Bible, and worshiped together as a household.

The church was meant to reinforce parents as spiritual trainers, Mark says, not replace them. It's time to stop outsourcing our children's futures and help our kids to love the values—and the Person—we love.

After viewing the DVD, use questions like these to help you think through what you saw and heard.

1. Which of the following best reflects the tone of Mark's presentation? Why?
   - "The house is on fire!"
   - "There's nothing we can do."
   - "We're the victims of a conspiracy."
   - "We can beat this thing."
   - "We can't help but win."

2. Mark grew up on the grounds of a Bible camp. Everything there was intentionally centered on Jesus and spiritual training. Do you want your home to be like that? Why or why not?

3. Why are so many kids spiritually "on fire" at camp and lukewarm at home? What percentage of the responsibility would you assign each of the following?
   - parents
   - the church
   - Satan
   - the kids themselves
   - the culture
   - peers
   - other _____

4. Are most young adults who stop attending church also giving up faith in Christ? Is it the same thing? Why or why not?

5. When young people say they left the church because of hypocrisy, which of the following do you think they mean?
   - They're disgusted by the scandals of church "leaders."
   - They're overwhelmed by guilt over their own two-faced behavior.

- They saw phoniness in their own parents and other adults.
- other _____

6. Which of the following has been most like your experience? What have you learned from it that influences the way you approach training your children spiritually?
    - You were raised in the church and never left.
    - You left but came back.
    - You still show up, but mentally checked out a long time ago.
    - other _____

7. Read Deuteronomy 6:1-9. Why doesn't this passage mention the church's role in spiritual training? How would you rank the influence (from most to least) of the following factors in these verses on the way kids "turn out"?
    - parents not talking about God's commands at home
    - parents not obeying the commands
    - parents not putting the commands on their hands and foreheads
    - parents not having the commands "on their hearts"
    - parents not writing the commands on their doorframes and gates
    - parents not loving God with all their heart, soul, and strength

8. If you asked your children who you're in love with, what do you think they'd say? If Mark Holmen is right in believing that our kids will love what we love, is that good news or bad news?

9. Mark has admitted "straying" spiritually, but came back because his parents stayed in the faith. Do parents have a lifelong responsibility to be role models so that their kids don't leave the church as adults? Why or why not?

Bible Study

> *Listen, my son, to your father's instruction*
> *and do not forsake your mother's teaching.*
> *They will be a garland to grace your head*
> *and a chain to adorn your neck. (Proverbs 1:8-9)*

1. Based on this passage, would you say that spiritual training is a job for dads only? Why or why not?

   Why do you suppose King Solomon bothered to explain why his son should listen to his parents' spiritual guidance? Why not just order the son to listen?

> *My son, do not forget my teaching,*
> *but keep my commands in your heart,*
> *for they will prolong your life many years*
> *and bring you prosperity.*
> *Let love and faithfulness never leave you;*
> *bind them around your neck,*
> *write them on the tablet of your heart.*
> *(Proverbs 3:1-3)*

2. What two reasons does Solomon give for following his instructions?

   If spiritually training your child will bring him or her the same benefits, is it worth your effort? Why or why not?

> *And my God will meet all your needs according to his glorious riches in Christ Jesus. (Philippians 4:19)*

3. As you consider helping your child to grow spiritually, which of the following is your greatest need?

____ time

____ energy

____ know-how

____ motivation

____ courage

____ other _____

Do you believe God can meet that need? Why or why not?

Being confident of this, that he who began a good work in you will carry it on to completion until the day of Christ Jesus. (Philippians 1:6)

4. What kind of "good work" has God started in your child's life so far?

What kind of person do you hope your child will be when that work is completed?

If God is calling you to train your child spiritually, can you trust Him to complete that process, too? Why or why not?

5. If you had to choose one of the previous verses as your "spiritual training motto," which would it be? Why?

Applying the Principles

1. One part of spiritual training is being a role model. On a scale of 1 to 10 (1 being horrified, 10 being ecstatic), circle a number to show

how happy you'd be if your son or daughter imitated your habits in each of the following areas:

HANDLING ANGER	1 2 3 4 5 6 7 8 9 10
GAMBLING	1 2 3 4 5 6 7 8 9 10
DRIVING	1 2 3 4 5 6 7 8 9 10
ALCOHOL USE	1 2 3 4 5 6 7 8 9 10
SEXUAL BEHAVIOR	1 2 3 4 5 6 7 8 9 10
DRESS	1 2 3 4 5 6 7 8 9 10
WORK HOURS	1 2 3 4 5 6 7 8 9 10
CREDIT CARD DEBT	1 2 3 4 5 6 7 8 9 10

2. Now ask yourself about behaviors you want your child to imitate. In each of the following areas, try to name an action you've taken in the last six months. Then indicate whether your child knows about it. (Note: If you're thinking that performing good deeds in front of others in order to win their praise is hypocritical, you're right [Matthew 6:1-6]. But the point of letting your child see these actions is to teach him or her to follow in your footsteps.)

SHARING YOUR FAITH
An action you took:
Does your child know about it?   ___ YES   ___ NO

FORGIVING
An action you took:
Does your child know about it?   ___ YES   ___ NO

PRAYING
An action you took:
Does your child know about it?   ___ YES   ___ NO

Based on your answers, which of the following do you need to work on more?

    ____ putting your faith into action

    ____ letting your child see you acting on your faith

3. When it comes to guiding your child spiritually, do you fear you have nothing to share? Maybe you're not as unqualified as you think.

   What's one aspect of the Christian life that you know a *little* more about than your child does?

   What's a spiritual mistake you've made that your child hasn't made yet?

   What did you learn from it that you could pass on to your child?

   Have you made even a *tiny* bit of progress since beginning your relationship with God?

   If so, what could you tell your child about that?

4. If you're afraid that it's too late to start training your child, please answer the following.

   Approximately how many days are left until your child graduates from high school?

   If you had to choose three things to accomplish in that time, which of the following would they be?

       ____ helping your child establish the habit of regular prayer and Bible reading

___ showing him or her why the Bible is reliable

___ getting your child to memorize a dozen key passages of Scripture

___ making sure he or she has a personal relationship with Christ

___ getting him or her to meet the needs of other people

___ other _____

If you had to choose just two of those things to accomplish, which would they be?

If you had to choose just one of them, which would it be?

Insight for Your Week

Christian parents want to know what it takes to build a lasting faith in their children, a faith that can withstand the trials and temptations of this world. They ask, "What can I do to make sure my kids stay strong in the faith—that they pass the test?"

Capturing a teachable moment is one of the easiest methods to train your child in spiritual matters. These are moments when you are with your child and something occurs that offers an opportunity to teach something about God. It's as simple as paying attention to the world around you and presenting it from a godly viewpoint.

For example, if you see a beautiful tree growing near a lake or river, you can point it out and say to your child, "Isn't that tree magnificent? God says that people of faith are like that tree. Trees stay strong because they grow near the water. People stay strong when they grow closer to God. What other good things happen if you grow near God?"

Or if you are at the grocery store and you receive extra change back from the cashier, you point out the mistake to your child, saying, "God wants us to be people of integrity. Should I give this extra money back or should I keep it?"

If you're like most parents, you want your children to learn biblical principles and become spiritually aware of what God is doing in their lives. And you probably already know that lectures don't work, Sunday school lays a good foundation but isn't always memorable or life-changing, and family devotion time turns into family demoralization time if the material isn't fun and relevant.

Once you discover the power of the teachable moment, however, you will have a method to make a life-changing spiritual impact through everyday events. A teachable moment gives you the resource to make the Bible relevant to your children today, right now.

A teachable moment requires three simple ingredients. The first is a good relationship between the parent and child. Most positive learning occurs best inside a loving bond. Second, a teachable moment requires a catalyst such as the extra change in the example above. A catalyst is the conversation starter, the reason the teachable moment is occurring at that specific time and place. You can even design your own catalyst to teach your child a specific truth. Third, a teachable moment requires a biblical truth. The truth can be a Bible fact, a truth about God's character, or insights into living a life of faith.

Teachable moments can be used to affirm, encourage, correct, or equip your child in spiritual matters. They are the perfect way to catch your child doing something good. For example, if your child's teacher comments that he gets along well with other people, you can tell him later, "I'm proud of you for being a cooperative person at school. The Bible says that Jesus got along well with other people when He was young. You are following in His footsteps when you treat others with respect and kindness."

Teachable moments are perfect for the single parent who doesn't have a partner to help pass on a spiritual legacy. They can be incorporated into any family routine, no matter how busy. Teachable moments require no manuals, discussion guides, or preparation. In fact, they work best when you're just having plain old fun with your kids.

—Jim Weidmann and Marianne Hering[2]

Chapter 2

RAISING OUR CHILDREN LIKE GOD RAISES US

My oldest daughter, Christie, is an adult. She's making her way in the world, finding her career path. God is already using her in some very special ways.

But not long ago, I heard her say, "It's tough being a Casey."

At first I thought, *Where does she get off complaining about her family?*

But then her words made sense. The sobering part was that, until that moment, I hadn't realized the pressure she was feeling. She wasn't rejecting it, just acknowledging it. I listened as she told me how she felt the need to perform a certain way, or win at whatever she tried, to avoid feeling she'd failed.

I can see where she's coming from. I'm not famous, but through the years I suppose I've gained visibility in some circles. Our family has connections with a wide range of people around the country. So I can understand if she feels there's a reputation to live up to. It probably doesn't help that in my current position I'm regularly talking and writing about her and her siblings, either.

Christie and I had a long talk about how proud I am of her and always will be. I told her I love her unconditionally.

Consider your own kids. Are they feeling pressure to carry on the family business, attend a particular college, perform in the arts, excel at sports, or continue in some pursuit because it's your thing? Give them some breathing room.

It can be good for our kids to know we have high expectations. But it's up to you to be aware of what your child is going through as a result. You may want to come right out and ask, "Do you feel pressure to be a certain way because you're my son or daughter?" Or, "Am I putting expectations on you that aren't realistic?" You could even ask, "What is hard for you about being part of this family?"

—Carey Casey
CEO, National Center for Fathering[3]

Identifying Your Needs

1. A good definition of "grace" is
   ___ unmerited favor.
   ___ asking the blessing.
   ___ what you do when you're too tired to punish your kids.
   ___ other _____

2. God's grace to you has been most like
   ___ a refreshing rain.
   ___ a debt you can never repay.
   ___ a box of chocolates you don't want to share.
   ___ other _____

3. When your child makes a mistake,
   ___ you see it as an opportunity to practice your "snarly face."
   ___ you see it as an opportunity for both of you to grow.
   ___ you see it as an opportunity to post a video on YouTube.
   ___ other _____

4. When you show grace, it enables your child to
    ___ resume spiritual growth with a clean slate.
    ___ learn how to give grace to others.
    ___ get away with murder.
    ___ other _____

5. The opposite of grace is
    ___ legalism.
    ___ harshness.
    ___ clumsiness.
    ___ other _____

6. The last time you showed grace to your child
    ___ he showed you grace in return.
    ___ you regretted it for the rest of your life.
    ___ the Beatles were still together.
    ___ other _____

Watching and Discussing the DVD

In this DVD segment, author Tim Kimmel warns parents that effective spiritual training isn't likely to take place without grace. Fear-based parenting leads to legalism, overprotection, and condemnation—grace's opposite. Moms and dads who let fear run their lives risk raising kids who never really learn to love God and the lost people around them.

Instead of trying to control our kids through guilt and shame, we need to correct them and move on. The battle for our children isn't "out there" in the culture, it's in their hearts. That battle isn't won by filling their heads with theology and constantly reminding them of their shortcomings. It's won by loving them the way Jesus loves us.

After viewing the DVD, use questions like these to help you think through what you saw and heard.

1. Do you think most Christian parents provide the "spiritual stuff" their kids need? If not, which of the following reasons might account for that?
   - They don't feel qualified.
   - They can't find time.
   - They don't have the "spiritual stuff" themselves.
   - They're overwhelmed by the depravity in today's world.
   - other _____

2. Which three of the following are scariest to you as a parent? Do you tend to respond to them by isolating your kids, locking them down, trying to distract them, giving up, or something else?
   - the Internet
   - movies, TV, and music
   - dating
   - predators
   - criticism of Christians and the Bible

3. If you were in a restaurant with your family and overheard a lot of profanity from diners at a nearby table, which of the following would you do? What do you think Tim Kimmel would recommend?
   - ignore it
   - smite the evildoers with a bottle of ketchup
   - quietly move to a table further away
   - use it later as a teachable moment with your kids
   - other _____

4. Read John 3:16-17. Why does God want to save the world instead of condemning it? Which of the following actions do you think conflict with that goal? Why?
    • telling your kids not to play with a Muslim family down the street
    • blocking a cable TV channel that shows R-rated movies
    • making a joke about gay people at the dinner table
    • praying in family devotions for the defeat of a presidential candidate

5. Which of the following rules do you think are biblical, and which are a matter of personal taste? What's one rule in your household that you're not sure about?
    • Don't play with your food.
    • No giggling when we're asking the blessing.
    • You can't wear a shirt with writing on it to church.
    • Don't stack anything on top of a Bible.

6. Tim Kimmel believes that Jesus merges grace and truth together (John 1:14) like two metals in an alloy. How could upholding both grace and truth help a parent resolve the following situations?
    • Your child wants to buy an album with a "Parental Advisory" sticker.
    • Your child doesn't want to invite an "ugly" girl to her birthday party.
    • Your child has lost interest in church since his best friend died.

7. How could you handle the following situations without using guilt or shame? What might you say to correct your child and assure him or her that you and God are ready to help?
    • Your four-year-old son is asked to leave preschool for biting other children.

- Your 16-year-old daughter reveals that she's pregnant.
- Your eight-year-old son blurts out a racial slur in front of your parents.
- Your 17-year-old daughter misses the deadline to apply to community college.

8. What could happen if a family tried too hard to be grace-based? How could you tell whether you'd "gone off the deep end" in this area?

Bible Study

"Therefore, the kingdom of heaven is like a king who wanted to settle accounts with his servants. As he began the settlement, a man who owed him ten thousand talents was brought to him. Since he was not able to pay, the master ordered that he and his wife and his children and all that he had be sold to repay the debt.

"The servant fell on his knees before him. 'Be patient with me,' he begged, 'and I will pay back everything.' The servant's master took pity on him, canceled the debt and let him go.

"But when that servant went out, he found one of his fellow servants who owed him a hundred denarii. He grabbed him and began to choke him. 'Pay back what you owe me!' he demanded.

"His fellow servant fell to his knees and begged him, 'Be patient with me, and I will pay you back.'

"But he refused. Instead, he went off and had the man thrown into prison until he could pay the debt. When the other servants saw what had happened, they were greatly distressed and went and told their master everything that had happened.

"Then the master called the servant in. 'You wicked servant,' he said,

'I canceled all that debt of yours because you begged me to. Shouldn't you have had mercy on your fellow servant just as I had on you?' In anger his master turned him over to the jailers to be tortured, until he should pay back all he owed.

"This is how my heavenly Father will treat each of you unless you forgive your brother from your heart." (Matthew 18:23-35)

1. Who showed grace in this story, and who didn't?

In the following space, try retelling the story with a twist. The first servant is a parent; the master is the parent's boss; the fellow servant is the child.

While Peter was below in the courtyard, one of the servant girls of the high priest came by. When she saw Peter warming himself, she looked closely at him.

"You also were with that Nazarene, Jesus," she said.

But he denied it. "I don't know or understand what you're talking about," he said, and went out into the entryway. (Mark 14:66-68)

2. On a scale of 1 to 10 (10 being highest), how serious an offense do you think it was for Peter to deny Jesus?

If a friend had done this to you, would you forgive him? Why or why not?

This was now the third time Jesus appeared to his disciples after he was raised from the dead.

When they had finished eating, Jesus said to Simon Peter, "Simon son of John, do you truly love me more than these?"

"Yes, Lord," he said, "you know that I love you."

Jesus said, "Feed my lambs." (John 21:14-15)

This took place after Peter's denial and Jesus' death. How did Jesus demonstrate grace here?

Why do you suppose Jesus gave Peter an assignment? Why not just say "I forgive you" and put him on probation?

If this conversation hadn't taken place, what do you think the rest of Peter's life would have been like?

But God demonstrates his own love for us in this: While we were still sinners, Christ died for us. (Romans 5:8)

We love because he first loved us. (1 John 4:19)

3. How could you make the first move in showing grace to your child—even though he or she might not deserve it?

Applying the Principles

1. Which of the following could help you feel God's grace toward you?

___ reading more about it in the Bible

___ watching a movie about Christ's sacrifice on the cross

____ thinking about some of your sins He's forgiven

____ listening to songs like "Amazing Grace" and "Your Grace Is Enough"

____ other _____

Which of those steps will you take this week?

2. In which of these areas has your child seemed to let you down during the last year?

____ behavior at school

____ telling the truth

____ competing in sports

____ spiritual growth

____ other _____

3. What would your child have to do before you could forgive him or her for letting you down?

____ Apologize.

____ Earn back my trust.

____ Change his or her behavior.

____ Suffer a penalty.

____ Nothing.

____ Other _____

4. How does your answer to the previous question compare with what you know of God's attitude toward forgiving you?

5. If your child asked for a "second chance," which of the following would it most likely be?

____ to play video games again after exceeding limits you'd set

___ to go out again after breaking curfew
___ to regain your trust after telling a lie
___ to use the computer after going to forbidden Web sites
___ other _____

If you gave your child that second chance, what do you think he or she would do with it?

If you're willing to grant that second chance, how will you announce it?

6. Which of these new beginnings would you most like to give your child by showing him grace?
    ___ being able to approach God without feeling guilty
    ___ being able to approach you without feeling condemned
    ___ being able to dream big dreams
    ___ being able to share his faith without feeling like a hypocrite
    ___ other _____

What's one step you can take this week toward that goal?

Insight for Your Week

On a beautiful summer day at an outdoor carnival, a mother scolded her four-year-old daughter for being too frightened to get on a Ferris wheel. "Honestly," she said, "I wonder why I bother with you at all. You're ruining the whole day."

An outsider might point out that the day still had many possibilities: the basketball throw; the petting zoo; a nice slow train ride; or a big, fluffy wad of cotton candy. Why judge the entire carnival on the basis of one event? Just like a turn on the Ferris wheel, that will get you nowhere.

It's natural for parents to have expectations for their children, but it becomes damaging to a relationship when specific expectations or criteria become the only measure of success. From a relationship perspective, that will get you nowhere. If the child measures up, he'll resent the pressure. If he doesn't measure up, the pain of the parent's rejection may last a lifetime.

Thirty-four-year-old Mike E.'s father never could accept his son's acne, for example. After a recent visit home to see his parents, Mike recalled the way his father introduced him to a golf buddy: "This here is my son, Mike. I never could get him to wash his face. That's why he's got those pitted scars." Talk about scars—Mike's emotional pain runs deep; he never felt accepted by his father because he wasn't handsome physically. Though Mike has become a successful and caring high school principal, he still longs to be cared for by his father.

God made your child for a unique purpose; learn to appreciate what good qualities your child has instead of dwelling on the areas where he or she disappoints you or is not like you. Let your kids lead you into the areas they have an interest in and you will see their good qualities shine.

I (Jim) was born and raised in a locker room. But neither of my sons is athletic. They are not built mentally or physically for football. When I realized that, I thought, *What am I going to do now? If I try to get my boys into my world, football, they will be killed.* Football would have set them up for failure, and I knew my relationship with them would suffer as a result.

So instead of hoping my boys would one day be scouted for a pro football team, I let them be scouts—Boy Scouts. Once a month

I entered the wilderness with 40 boys armed with knives. I got it all: wind, rain, snow, blisters, and bears. I had a great time with my boys.

If they had pursued football, they would have felt they could not meet my expectations, and as a result, they would never feel they had my approval. They would not feel like they received my blessing. The Boy Scouts helped them to learn self-control and discipline. It also helped us discover each other. What I didn't count on from the experience was that my Jacob and Joshua would develop this internal pride that their dad was scoutmaster. They received my approval and blessing—and I received theirs.

If your child feels loved just the way he is, then he'll be more willing to believe that God loves him, which is the first step toward a healthy spiritual relationship. If he feels accepted by you, he will probably accept a teachable moment when it is offered.

—Jim Weidmann and Marianne Hering[4]

Chapter 3

THE DRIVING NEEDS OF OUR CHILDREN

I wear two rings on my body every day.

One is a golden band that reminds me constantly of the promises I made to my bride. Before I slipped that ring on her finger and she slipped one on mine, we promised to love and cherish one another.

The other ring I wear is a blue rubber wristband—available at fathers.com—inscribed with those three little words: *Loving, Coaching,* and *Modeling.*

My wedding ring is valuable and unchanging. The vows I made the day Melanie and I became husband and wife were intended to be precious and enduring—like gold.

The rubber ring on my wrist represents my promises to my children and the special aspects of our relationship. The material it's made of reminds me that I can expect to be stretched by my kids. It drives home the point that being a dad is a call to be flexible. If I'm *inflexible* and my children stretch me (because that's what children do whether they want to or not), then something's got to give—and not in a good way!

Being a loving father is a demanding balance between firmness and flexibility. My kids (and my bride) need to know that there are some solid, unchanging things about me—the core of who I am as a man, husband, and dad. They also need to know that I can flex with life; that I'm learning, too; and that even though I haven't got everything figured out, I'm on my way.

One thing my wedding ring and the wristband share in common:
Neither will break. I want my kids to understand that. It shapes the way
in which my family experiences love from me.

—Carey Casey
CEO, National Center for Fathering[5]

Identifying Your Needs

Take a couple of minutes to fill out the following survey.

1. The idea that parents are "hardwired" to love their children is
   ___ a myth.
   ___ sad but true.
   ___ like saying sumo wrestlers are a bit pudgy.
   ___ other _____

2. The hardest part of loving your kids is
   ___ shepherding them through their daily emotional
       struggles.
   ___ helping them to form their own identities.
   ___ not being able to sleep through the whole thing.
   ___ other _____

3. How do you prefer to express affection to your child?
   ___ through words
   ___ through touch
   ___ from a distance of at least 12 miles
   ___ other _____

4. If you try to impose rules without having a good relationship with your child, you'll get

___ rich.

___ rebellion.

___ on one of those awful daytime TV talk shows.

___ other _____

5. Your child knows you love her because

___ you say it every day.

___ you demonstrate it every day.

___ your people faxed her people a document to that effect.

___ other _____

6. The difference between God's love for you and your love for your child is

___ the difference between lightning and the lightning bug.

___ immeasurable.

___ very slight, except that yours is conditional, selfish, and totally depraved.

___ other _____

Watching and Discussing the DVD

The day-to-day roller coaster of raising kids can make you queasy. But what about the long-term journey? Exactly where is that roller coaster taking you and your child?

In this video segment, author Tim Kimmel takes a big-picture view of parenting. What are our children's greatest needs? What are kids here for? What happens when their needs aren't met and they don't understand what God has in mind for their lives?

Tim urges parents to do four things: create an atmosphere of grace; provide love, security, and purpose; build character; and aim for true greatness instead of mere "success." Rather than trying to raise kids who are only good-looking, smart, or biblically savvy, we need to bring up children who are strong enough to face whatever comes their way.

After viewing the DVD, use questions like these to help you think through what you saw and heard.

1. The Kimmels told their children to "Go glow in the darkness" as lights of the world. Which of the following comes closest to the long-range directions you'd give your kids? Why?
   - "Let's be careful out there."
   - "Don't let the bedbugs bite."
   - "Buy low, sell high."
   - "Don't call us, we'll call you."
   - other _____

2. Tim urges parents to create an "atmosphere of grace" at home, giving kids the freedom to be who God wants them to be. What are three ways in which parents can help their children discover those God-given identities?

3. Kids need to know they're loved, even when they're hard to love. In each of the following situations, how would you let your child know he or she is loved?
   - Your teenage son hasn't taken a shower in a week.
   - Your baby has colic and seems to have been crying constantly for the last four months.

- Your fifth grader is in a terrible mood, having just "lost the game" for his softball team.
- Your seventh-grade daughter is mad because you won't let her get her nose pierced.

4. Which of the following would probably help a child feel more secure, but not a parent? Which might help a parent feel more secure, but not a child? Which could help both?
   - having a six-month "cushion" in your bank account
   - setting a 9 p.m. curfew for a junior in high school
   - asking a teenager to make an abstinence pledge
   - telling a two-year-old not to cross the street alone

5. In five words or less, how would you describe the life purpose of each of the following? How might the world be different if these people had never been born?
   - Dr. Martin Luther King, Jr.
   - the apostle Paul
   - Ruth Bell Graham
   - your child

6. Which of the following would you call internal character building? Which would you call external "sin management"? Why?
   - getting rid of your family's TV
   - interviewing any young man who wants to date your daughter
   - paying your kids to memorize Bible verses

7. What's the difference between "true greatness" and the "success" of fame, fortune, and good looks? Who are two living people you could hold up to your child as examples of true greatness?

Bible Study

> *And God spoke all these words:*
> *"I am the LORD your God, who brought you out of Egypt, out of the*
> *land of slavery.*
> *"You shall have no other gods before me.*
> *"You shall not make for yourself an idol in the form of anything in*
> *heaven above or on the earth beneath or in the waters below. You shall*
> *not bow down to them or worship them; for I, the LORD your God, am a*
> *jealous God, punishing the children for the sin of the fathers to the third*
> *and fourth generation of those who hate me, but showing love to a thou-*
> *sand [generations] of those who love me and keep my commandments."*
> *(Exodus 20:1-6)*

1. In this passage, how does God remind the Israelites of His relationship with them before "laying down the law"?

   What kind of relationship with your child would you like to establish before "laying down the rules"?

2. For each of the following verses, circle the words and phrases that are easiest for you to practice in your relationship with your child. Then underline the ones that are hardest.

   > *Be devoted to one another in brotherly love. Honor one another*
   > *above yourselves. (Romans 12:10)*

   > *Live in harmony with one another. Do not be proud, but be willing to*
   > *associate with people of low position. Do not be conceited. (Romans 12:16)*

Let no debt remain outstanding, except the continuing debt to love one another, for he who loves his fellowman has fulfilled the law. (Romans 13:8)

Therefore let us stop passing judgment on one another. Instead, make up your mind not to put any stumbling block or obstacle in your brother's way. (Romans 14:13)

Accept one another, then, just as Christ accepted you, in order to bring praise to God. (Romans 15:7)

You, my brothers, were called to be free. But do not use your freedom to indulge the sinful nature; rather, serve one another in love. (Galatians 5:13)

Be completely humble and gentle; be patient, bearing with one another in love. (Ephesians 4:2)

Be kind and compassionate to one another, forgiving each other, just as in Christ God forgave you. (Ephesians 4:32)

Submit to one another out of reverence for Christ. (Ephesians 5:21)

Bear with each other and forgive whatever grievances you may have against one another. Forgive as the Lord forgave you. (Colossians 3:13)

3. Read the following verse. When was the last time you felt exasperated by someone? How did it affect your relationship?

Fathers, do not exasperate your children; instead, bring them up in the training and instruction of the Lord. (Ephesians 6:4)

How can you tell from this verse that spiritual training should not, in itself, exasperate your child?

If spiritual training seems to be a negative experience for your child, what might be the cause?

Applying the Principles

How are you doing with Tim Kimmel's idea of grace-based parenting? To help you measure your progress, let's compare it to painting the rooms of your home. You've got 10 kinds of paint, stain, and wood preservative to work with. Some, like "Security Scarlet," promote a grace-based family; others, like "Fear-Based Fuschia," don't.

How much of each can have you used so far? How much do you want to use in the coming year? Write the percentages next to each can.

PERCENTAGE OF THIS COLOR THAT YOU'VE USED IN THE "ROOMS" OF YOUR HOME _____

PERCENTAGE OF THIS COLOR THAT YOU WANT TO USE IN THE COMING YEAR _____

PERCENTAGE OF THIS COLOR THAT YOU'VE USED IN THE "ROOMS" OF YOUR HOME _____

PERCENTAGE OF THIS COLOR THAT YOU WANT TO USE IN THE COMING YEAR _____

PERCENTAGE OF THIS COLOR THAT YOU'VE
USED IN THE "ROOMS" OF YOUR HOME _____

PERCENTAGE OF THIS COLOR THAT YOU
WANT TO USE IN THE COMING YEAR _____

PERCENTAGE OF THIS COLOR THAT YOU'VE
USED IN THE "ROOMS" OF YOUR HOME _____

PERCENTAGE OF THIS COLOR THAT YOU
WANT TO USE IN THE COMING YEAR _____

PERCENTAGE OF THIS COLOR THAT YOU'VE
USED IN THE "ROOMS" OF YOUR HOME _____

PERCENTAGE OF THIS COLOR THAT YOU
WANT TO USE IN THE COMING YEAR _____

PERCENTAGE OF THIS COLOR THAT YOU'VE
USED IN THE "ROOMS" OF YOUR HOME _____

PERCENTAGE OF THIS COLOR THAT YOU
WANT TO USE IN THE COMING YEAR _____

PERCENTAGE OF THIS COLOR THAT YOU'VE
USED IN THE "ROOMS" OF YOUR HOME _____

PERCENTAGE OF THIS COLOR THAT YOU
WANT TO USE IN THE COMING YEAR _____

 PERCENTAGE OF THIS COLOR THAT YOU'VE USED IN THE "ROOMS" OF YOUR HOME _____

PERCENTAGE OF THIS COLOR THAT YOU WANT TO USE IN THE COMING YEAR _____

 PERCENTAGE OF THIS COLOR THAT YOU'VE USED IN THE "ROOMS" OF YOUR HOME _____

PERCENTAGE OF THIS COLOR THAT YOU WANT TO USE IN THE COMING YEAR _____

 PERCENTAGE OF THIS COLOR THAT YOU'VE USED IN THE "ROOMS" OF YOUR HOME _____

PERCENTAGE OF THIS COLOR THAT YOU WANT TO USE IN THE COMING YEAR _____

Now ask yourself: Judging from your percentages, are you especially fond of some of these colors? How do you feel about that? Would you like to change anything about the "color scheme" in your home? If so, how?

Insight for Your Week

If you want to make a spiritual impact on your child, you need to know the answer to the following riddle.

Q: How do you spell love?

A: T-I-M-E.

Several years ago, *Focus on the Family Clubhouse®* magazine asked kids to send in ideas for helpful inventions to give their dads. The editors expected to receive some wacky suggestions for golf gizmos or automatic nose hair pluckers, but what poured in were ideas for machines that would do Dad's work so he could be at home more often. What was intended as a lighthearted question revealed that the readers had heavy hearts: The children longed to spend more time with their fathers.

Britney, age eight, from Bumpass, Virginia, wrote: "With this carpenter machine, my dad can take a day off and send this robot to work." An 11-year-old physician's son said, "I would invent a robot surgeon to help my dad get his work done more quickly so he can come home earlier." And the most poignant of the lot: "Since I am not around to give my dad hugs, I would create a gizmo that would give him hugs and make him feel good."

The responses *Clubhouse* received were aimed at dads because it was a Father's Day magazine issue, but kids need their moms, too. Because an estimated 72 percent of mothers with children under age 18 work outside the home, we can assume that children would create similar work-reducing inventions so that Mom can also have more time at home.

Our children need and want time with both their parents. Are you there for yours? To assess your baseline Availability Score, take this short quiz about the last seven days' family activities. If you're a parent with a job that requires travel, or a divorced or separated parent with only partial custody, modify the time span to reflect the last week you lived with your child or, if you see him or her only on weekends, the last month.

1. I ate at least three meals with my children last week.

    ___Yes ___No

2. During the last seven days, I made sure that I spent at least one hour alone with each of my children.
   ___Yes ___No

3. I can tell you what clothes my children wore yesterday (without searching the laundry basket or looking under their beds for clues).
   ___Yes ___No

4. If I asked my children right now, they would say that last week we had at least one fun family time together.
   ___Yes ___No

5. The last time I ran errands, I took a child with me.
   ___Yes ___No

6. In the last seven days I helped my oldest child with a hobby, homework, or sports activity.
   ___Yes ___No

7. I tucked my youngest child into bed at least twice this week.
   ___Yes ___No

8. I went on a "date" with one of my children last week.
   ___Yes ___No

9. I have given each of my children at least three compliments over the last seven days.
   ___Yes ___No

10. My children know about and are looking forward to our next scheduled family activity.
    ___Yes ___No

11. I know the names of each of my children's "best" friends this week, and I know the names of the people they ate lunch with.
    ___Yes ___No

12. I know the names of my children's Sunday school teachers as well as their academic teachers.
    ___Yes ___No

13. I hugged each of my children every day last week.
    ___Yes ___No

Tally the number of "yes" answers and check out your score:

0 to 4: Is this a hint that you may not be spending enough time with your children?

5 to 9: You probably clock in enough hours at home, but you may need to intentionally develop your parent-child relationships.

10 to 13: You're there; you're doing the right things. Good job.

—Jim Weidmann and Marianne Hering[6]

Chapter 4

YOUR FAMILY'S FAITH PLAN

My Pop worked in a Veteran's Administration hospital. But he thought of himself as a philosopher. He liked to lay profound thoughts on us kids, then observe as we tried to figure them out.

One of his favorite words was "watch." He'd say, "Son, you must always *watch*."

The first time he did that, there was something in his tone that caught my attention. "C'mon, Pop," I said. "What do you mean, 'watch'? School me, Dad."

It turned out that "watch" was his way of saying, "Be careful. Don't take life lightly. Don't get hurt because you weren't paying attention to something important."

Usually we'd hear this when someone had gotten us in trouble. Pop would tell us, "Son, watch. Don't be in the wrong place at the wrong time and get your car shot at." Or, "Watch! Don't be at some party where you don't need to be. Watch!"

We also heard it when others made tragic mistakes. A young man in my hometown, one of the greatest athletes ever to come up, drowned in the river his senior year because he underestimated the currents. "Watch," Pop told us.

A few years later, my cousin took off in his car late one night to meet some girls, even after his father told him it wasn't a good idea. He missed a turn, and it ended his life. "He wasn't watching," my dad said.

Back then I got tired of hearing it. Today, though, I see the value of his speaking truth into my life. He saved me from difficult times and big regrets. Reminding me to "watch" was a form of coaching.

That kind of guidance has a way of becoming part of a family's fiber. I noticed that one day several years ago, when I visited my daughter Patrice at college. As I left her dorm room, I saw that word, boldly typed and taped above the doorknob: "Watch." She valued that word from my dad, and wanted to be reminded each time she walked out that door.

Like my Pop, you have lessons you've learned. How will you pass them on?

—Carey Casey
CEO, National Center for Fathering[7]

Identifying Your Needs

Here's a survey; please take a few minutes to fill it out.

1. You know the Old Testament story of Joseph as well as you know
   ____ the back of your hand.
   ____ the back of your head.
   ____ the Urdu translation of the Periodic Table of Elements.
   ____ other _____

2. Which of the following could be called the "anti-Joseph"?
   ____ the brothers who threw him into a well

___ the Prodigal Son

___ a guy with a Coat of One Color

___ other _____

3. If you wanted to teach your child about wisdom and foolishness, you'd use the examples of

___ Joseph and the Prodigal Son.

___ the Tortoise and the Hare.

___ Ned Flanders and Homer Simpson.

___ other _____

4. If you were the Prodigal Son's father, you would

___ welcome him home with open arms.

___ give him a stern lecture and a stale bagel.

___ have him arrested for trespassing and let the fatted calf live in his room.

___ other _____

5. Your child would be most interested in

___ Joseph's ability to interpret dreams.

___ Joseph's ability to resist temptation.

___ Joseph's ability to annoy his siblings.

___ other _____

6. The secret of Joseph's success was

___ his good looks.

___ his spiritual training.

___ knowing he would someday be the star of an Andrew Lloyd Webber musical.

___ other _____

Watching and Discussing the DVD

Joseph from the Old Testament was a colorful character—and not just because of his Technicolor dreamcoat. At age 17, this handsome visionary involuntarily entered a pagan culture where he had no support system and faced temptation daily. Through it all, he stayed faithful to God and rose to national prominence.

As our kids prepare to enter a world with some striking similarities, most of us hope they'll stand for God as Joseph did. But can we do more than hope?

Larry Fowler, author of *Raising a Modern-Day Joseph* (David C. Cook, 2009), says we can. In this DVD segment, he calls parents to be intentional about raising modern-day Josephs, aiming for clear spiritual-growth goals.

After viewing the DVD, use questions like these to help you think through what you saw and heard.

1. How have you had to "let go" of your child so far? What were you afraid might happen? Did the experience make you less fearful about the next "letting go" you face? Why or why not?

2. The Bible doesn't say much about the upbringing of Joseph or the Prodigal Son. Since they turned out so differently after leaving home, what might most people assume about the way they were raised? Would it be fair to assume that? Why or why not?

3. According to Larry Fowler's statistics, if you're an average Christian parent and have two children, one of them probably will walk away from the church—at least temporarily. Which of the following comes closest to your reaction?
   - "They'll be back."
   - "It won't happen to my kid."

- "I feel powerless."
- "I'd better start praying now."

4. Which of the following tend to get a higher priority in your home than spiritual training does? Why?
   - homework
   - sports
   - TV, Internet, music
   - friends
   - chores

5. Larry Fowler believes most of us aren't specific enough about the ways in which we'd like our kids to grow spiritually. Which of the following measurements do you think would be helpful in setting your spiritual-training goals? Why?
   - number of prayers prayed per day
   - number of Bible verses memorized per month
   - number of church events attended per week
   - number of service projects participated in per year
   - other _____

6. What are three things you'd like to be able to say about your child when he or she is 30 years old? What are three things that would cause you to grieve if you had to say them about your child at age 30?

7. Larry believes the home is most important in spiritual training because that's where grace is given and received, and it's where the heart is formed. If these things aren't happening in your home, should you wait to begin spiritual training until they are? Why or why not?

8. Larry encourages parents to make a connection between long-range spiritual goals and everyday activities. How might you use the following activities to reach your long-range spiritual goals?

- feeding a pet
- calling or e-mailing a grandparent
- grocery shopping
- after-school snacks
- driving home from church

Bible Study

Each of the following passages hints at one or more goals God has for every believer—including your child. After each passage, list all the goals you can find.

> *For those God foreknew he also predestined to be conformed to the likeness of his Son, that he might be the firstborn among many brothers. (Romans 8:29)*

1. The goal(s):

> *And he made known to us the mystery of his will according to his good pleasure, which he purposed in Christ, to be put into effect when the times will have reached their fulfillment—to bring all things in heaven and on earth together under one head, even Christ. (Ephesians 1:9-10)*

2. The goal(s):

> *Now the Bereans were of more noble character than the Thessalonians, for they received the message with great eagerness and examined the Scriptures every day to see if what Paul said was true. (Acts 17:11)*

3. The goal(s):

> *I want to know Christ and the power of his resurrection and the fellowship of sharing in his sufferings, becoming like him in his death, and so, somehow, to attain to the resurrection from the dead. (Philippians 3:10-11)*

4. The goal(s):

> *Hearing that Jesus had silenced the Sadducees, the Pharisees got together. One of them, an expert in the law, tested him with this question: "Teacher, which is the greatest commandment in the Law?" Jesus replied: "'Love the Lord your God with all your heart and with all your soul and with all your mind.' This is the first and greatest commandment. And the second is like it: 'Love your neighbor as yourself.' All the Law and the Prophets hang on these two commandments." (Matthew 22:34-40)*

5. The goal(s):

> *But the fruit of the Spirit is love, joy, peace, patience, kindness, goodness, faithfulness, gentleness and self-control. Against such things there is no law. (Galatians 5:22-23)*

6. The goal(s):

> *He has showed you, O man, what is good.*
> *And what does the LORD require of you?*
> *To act justly and to love mercy*
> *and to walk humbly with your God. (Micah 6:8)*

7. The goal(s):

Applying the Principles

1. What are your goals for spiritually training your child? Here are some ideas to get you started. Add one of your own to the last of the following targets.

   A Personal, Vibrant Relationship with Jesus Christ

   A Head Filled with Applied Wisdom from Scripture

   Skill in Filtering Life Through a Christian Worldview

   An Ability to Articulate and Defend the Bible

Wanting to Make Christ Known Through Life, Work, Service, and Witness

Other _____

Now make an "X" on each target to show how close you think your child is to a "bull's-eye."

2. Which of the following is true for your child?

___ You know when he began a personal relationship with Christ.

___ You believe he has such a relationship because of the way he acts.

___ You aren't sure whether he has such a relationship.

___ You doubt he has such a relationship.

Based on your answer, which of these is most urgent?

___ Asking your child whether he has a personal relationship with Christ.

___ Asking whether he would like to begin such a relationship.

___ Asking how that relationship has grown since it began.

___ Building a level of honesty that enables you to ask questions like these.

3. Which of the following do you think your child can quote? Indicate the percentage of accuracy you believe she would achieve for each passage.

THE LORD'S PRAYER
100%   75%   50%   25%   0%

THE TEN COMMANDMENTS
100%   75%   50%   25%   0%

THE FRUIT OF THE SPIRIT (Galatians 5:22-23)
100%   75%   50%   25%   0%

PSALM 23
100%   75%   50%   25%   0%

THE BEATITUDES (Matthew 5:3-12)
100%   75%   50%   25%   0%

JOHN 3:16
100%   75%   50%   25%   0%

Try testing your child this week to see how correct your answers were.

Now circle the percentages that indicate how well you think your child *understands* the Bible passages.

Finally, underline the percentages that show how well you think your child has *applied* the principles of each passage to her life.

Based on your answers, do you need to work most with your child on memorizing, understanding, or obeying the Bible?

4. In which two of the following areas do you think your child is least likely to have a "Christian worldview"?

___ entertainment choices

___ sharing with others

___ caring for God's creation

___ attitude toward teachers

___ church attendance

___ career plans

___ obeying parents

Based on your answers, which of these areas do you need to work on most?

Insight for Your Week

You can turn negative catalysts into positive teaching times.

Youth speaker Josh McDowell tells how one day he sat with his kids in a public place that had been vandalized by offensive graffiti. Instead of trying to shield them from the profanity and quickly ushering them to more neutral territory, he pointed it out to them. He answered their questions about the "colorful" language and helped them identify the artist's distorted values.

Josh hadn't planned to deliver an object lesson that day. But when the opportunity presented itself, he took full advantage of it.

Even life's little disasters can provide chances to create a strong teachable moment. Hannah recalls what happened when she was 15.

I tried to sneak the family car out of the garage late at night. I planned to have it back before anyone noticed, and I guess I was thinking too far ahead or something. I went to back out, but it didn't go backward. It went forward instead, right through the wall of my sister's bedroom. Luckily, she was away at college. But I just shut off the car and started crying. My dad came out and saw me, but if he was angry, he didn't show it. He made sure I was all right and helped me get the car back in the garage. Then, over the next few months, he rebuilt the wall and we actually repainted the room together.

Hannah's dad made that time count. His response left her with a lasting image of her father's love and patience that she'll never forget.

Sometimes things happen in the world around us that must be addressed through a teachable moment, even if you feel your child isn't ready or even if you're not ready.

Kurt Bruner, former vice president of resource development at Focus on the Family, was eating his breakfast when his son Kyle, then 11, gave him some more to chew on. "Can I have the paper for the horoscope section?"

Holding back a choking cough, Kurt said, "Why do you want that?"

"I have an assignment for school where we have to write a horoscope."

Kurt became agitated, and at first Kyle thought he had done something wrong. After reassuring Kyle that he wasn't in trouble, Kurt began a discussion about what horoscopes and divination are, even though Kurt would have liked to wait until Kyle was older. He told Kyle that those things try to take the place of God's wisdom, to answer questions that only God can and should answer. Then Kurt had a subsequent "teachable moment" with Kyle's teacher.

This type of catalyst is a mini-crisis. While you have no choice but to explain the death of a sibling or address the fact that your house has burned down, you can choose to ignore the milder crises that come your way. Kurt could have told his son to "never mind" the horoscope project and dealt only with the teacher. But unless your child is very young, it is foolish to gloss over something because it creates a "forbidden" or "grown-up" aura. Skirting the issue sends a message that this subject is not to be discussed at home. As a result, when your child needs information about it, he or she may not turn to you but rather to another source of information, such as peers or the Internet. You need to ask yourself where you want your child learning about drugs, sex, homosexuality, or Ouija boards.

That doesn't mean if your seven-year-old child wants to know about demon possession that you rent *The Exorcist* and watch it together. You need only to satisfy his or her curiosity with age-appropriate material, starting with the biblical perspective.

—Jim Weidmann and Marianne Hering[8]

Chapter 5

TOOLS FOR YOUR FAMILY'S FAITH PLAN

One of the biggest eye-openers in my life as a father happened when I was a young dad and pastor. My oldest child, Christie, was five; Patrice was three. It was Father's Day, and we were all getting ready for church.

I was in the living room, writing final notes for my Father's Day sermon. Christie knew it was a regular Sunday ritual for me to look over what I was going to preach. Running up and leaping on my lap, she asked, "Daddy, are you going to be a sermon today?"

She didn't mean it the way it came out. But I believe God speaks to us in mysterious ways, and He often uses the simple but powerful voices of our children.

That question became my sermon that morning—and has stayed with me ever since. I'll go to my grave remembering it.

It's a question I have to live up to every day. How about you? When you get down to it, are you modeling what you know is right, or just talking about it? Are you loving your children's mother? Are you really listening to your son or daughter? Is your life made up of patterns you'd be pleased for your kids to follow?

I'm finding it's much more important to my children that I *be* a sermon for them than preach one to them. We can *tell* our kids all day long how to live, but they're more likely to *do* what they see lived out day after day.

—Carey Casey
CEO, National Center for Fathering[9]

Identifying Your Needs

1. When you try to teach your kids to respect authority, you usually end up
   ___ throwing the book at them.
   ___ throwing up your hands in despair.
   ___ throwing up.
   ___ other _____

2. Which of the following best describes your child's attitude toward the Bible?
   ___ "God says it; I believe it; that settles it."
   ___ "Thy words are like an honeycomb unto my mouth."
   ___ "What comes after First Carbuncles?"
   ___ other _____

3. Your child learned all she knows about grace from
   ___ watching you forgive your spouse.
   ___ watching Aslan sacrifice himself in the first Chronicles of Narnia movie.
   ___ watching her step when you're in a bad mood.
   ___ other _____

4. Your parents prepared you to fulfill your destiny by
   ___ supporting you when you had doubts.
   ___ showing you how to answer skeptics.
   ___ locking you in the closet until you agreed with them.
   ___ other _____

5. You want your child to see life from a Christian perspective because
   ___ it leads to happiness.
   ___ all truth is God's truth.
   ___ you'd be embarrassed if he became an atheist.
   ___ other _____

6. If you could start over with spiritually training your child, you would
   ___ set higher goals.
   ___ set more realistic goals.
   ___ hire Larry Fowler to live in your basement.
   ___ other _____

Watching and Discussing the DVD

Author Larry Fowler continues his look at raising Christ-followers in this video segment. It's not enough, he says, to have a target for our training. We need a plan for hitting that target.

According to Larry, the Old Testament's Joseph was guided by five principles that can form a "life thread" to be woven throughout our training efforts:

1. Respect God's authority.

2. See God and His Word as the source of wisdom.

3. Receive God's grace and give grace to others.

4. Find your destiny, or purpose, in God's will.

5. Have the perspective that God is sovereign in everything.

The result: modern-day Josephs who stand fast when the world is crumbling around them.

After viewing the DVD, use questions like these to help you think through what you saw and heard.

1. Have the things you've taught your child so far added up to a "life thread"? If so, which of the following comes closest to describing it?
   - "You only go around once in life, so grab all the gusto you can."
   - "Life stinks, then you die."
   - "Only one life, 'twill soon be past; only what's done for Christ will last."
   - "Live like you were dyin'."
   - other _____

2. Which of the following probably would say you have a plan for meeting your spiritual training goals? Why?
   - your child
   - your spouse
   - you
   - God
   - Larry Fowler

3. What do you think Joseph would have thought of this DVD segment? Why?

4. What do you think the following people would like to teach your child about God's authority? How does their influence in your child's life compare with your own?
   - your child's favorite schoolteacher
   - the makers of video games like *Grand Theft Auto*
   - your child's Sunday school teacher
   - atheist authors like Richard Dawkins and Christopher Hitchens
   - your child's favorite recording artist

5. If you had to prove to your child that you believe God and His Word are the sources of wisdom, how would you do it? What evidence could be offered that might put your regard for Scripture in doubt?

6. When it comes to grace, is it better to give or receive? Why? In five words or less, what do you most want your child to know about God's grace?

7. Larry Fowler suggests that children need to find their destiny—their purpose—in God's will. Which of the following approaches to knowing God's will do you think you'll recommend when you talk with your kids about it? Why?
   - Pray.
   - Read the Bible.
   - Ask a mature believer.
   - Look for a "sign."
   - Take a wild guess.
   - other _____

8. How could you use the following situations to encourage your child to remember that God is always in charge?
   - Your child sees a severe thunderstorm warning on a TV newscast.
   - Your child's favorite uncle recovers after a major operation.
   - Your child enters a contest, hoping to win $100, but loses.

Bible Study

> He then brought them out and asked, "Sirs, what must I do to be saved?"
> They replied, "Believe in the Lord Jesus, and you will be saved—you and your household." (Acts 16:30-31)

1. Has your child taken this step? How do you know?

   If your answer to the previous question is yes, what are two other steps of faith you'd like to see your child take before leaving home?

   > *Then he told them many things in parables, saying: "A farmer went out to sow his seed. As he was scattering the seed, some fell along the path, and the birds came and ate it up. Some fell on rocky places, where it did not have much soil. It sprang up quickly, because the soil was shallow. But when the sun came up, the plants were scorched, and they withered because they had no root. Other seed fell among thorns, which grew up and choked the plants. Still other seed fell on good soil, where it produced a crop—a hundred, sixty or thirty times what was sown. He who has ears, let him hear."*
   >
   > *. . . "Listen then to what the parable of the sower means: When anyone hears the message about the kingdom and does not understand it, the evil one comes and snatches away what was sown in his heart. This is the seed sown along the path. The one who received the seed that fell on rocky places is the man who hears the word and at once receives it with joy. But since he has no root, he lasts only a short time. When trouble or persecution comes because of the word, he quickly falls away. The one who received the seed that fell among the thorns is the man who hears the word, but the worries of this life and the deceitfulness of wealth choke it, making it unfruitful. But the one who received the seed that fell on good soil is the man who hears the word and understands it. He produces a crop, yielding a hundred, sixty or thirty times what was sown." (Matthew 13:3-9, 18-23)*

2. According to this parable, what are three reasons why a person who seemed to start a relationship with God as a young child might no longer appear to have such a relationship?

What's one thing a parent can do to nurture the spiritual "seed" that's been planted in a young person's life?

> *What good is it, my brothers, if a man claims to have faith but has no deeds? Can such faith save him? Suppose a brother or sister is without clothes and daily food. If one of you says to him, "Go, I wish you well; keep warm and well fed," but does nothing about his physical needs, what good is it? In the same way, faith by itself, if it is not accompanied by action, is dead.*
>
> *But someone will say, "You have faith; I have deeds."*
>
> *Show me your faith without deeds, and I will show you my faith by what I do.*
>
> *You believe that there is one God. Good! Even the demons believe that—and shudder. (James 2:14-19)*

3. What are three actions your child has taken in the last year that indicate his or her faith is real?

    If you can't answer the previous question, how do you feel about that?

    > *Train a child in the way he should go,*
    > *and when he is old he will not turn from it. (Proverbs 22:6)*

4. Many commentators believe this verse is not a promise, but a statement of a principle that's generally true. Do you agree? Why or why not?

    If a child's spiritual training doesn't include the process of turning beliefs into personal convictions, what may happen when the child is "old"?

Applying the Principles

1. Which of the following "fruit" have you seen in your child's life during the last year?

____ increased interest in what the Bible has to say

____ concern for others

____ sharing faith with a friend

____ asking questions about spiritual things

____ wanting to spend more time with Christians

____ expressing enthusiasm about being a Christian

____ other _____

What does your answer lead you to conclude about your child's commitment to Christ?

Asking your child to tell you what Jesus means to him or her now may elicit a revealing answer—or a vague one. To encourage specific responses, try reading the following list of words aloud to your child this week. After each word, ask your child whether that word describes something about his or her relationship to Jesus today—and why.

GUILT	HAPPINESS	RULES
STRENGTH	LOVE	BORING
ADVENTURE	FORGIVENESS	HEAVEN
DOUBT	SACRIFICE	PUNISHMENT
HELP	RESCUE	OBEYING

2. Remember the "life thread" from Joseph's story? Here are five principles that made up that thread. They guided Joseph, and they can guide your child, too—if you teach them consistently. On each "strand" of the

thread, make a mark showing how well you think your child under-stands that principle. If your child is too young to grasp the concept, make a mark showing how well-prepared you feel to teach it. The left end of the thread represents zero; the right end stands for a "perfect ten."

Respect God's authority.

See God and His Word as the source of wisdom.

Receive God's grace and give grace to others.

Find your destiny (purpose) in God's will.

Have the perspective that God is sovereign in everything.

Based on the way you've marked these strands, what "loose ends" might you need to tie up?

Who might be able to help you with that task?

Insight for Your Week

Karie Hughes knows all about vulnerability and forgiveness. Feeling lonely and depressed after her divorce, she went to a nightclub, met a guy, and had a one-night stand. That one night led to months of guilt and shame as she carried an unwanted pregnancy to term and gave the baby up for adoption. Her two children, then ages four and seven, were wide-eyed witnesses to her pain.

To restore her credibility as a Christian with her children, she not only confessed to God and to them but she also became a counselor at a Christian family care agency, helping women in similar circumstances by sharing her experience of God's forgiveness.

If Karie hadn't been so honest, vulnerable, and visibly changed, her children would be able to accuse her of being a hypocrite and leave the faith. They would have an excuse to sin in the same way. But because her faults have been covered up by the faultlessness of Jesus, her relationship with her kids is strong.

Not all past sins can be detected so easily. What about those past or private sins we all have, the ones that no one else besides God would ever find out if we didn't share them? Why would we tell our own kids that we used illegal drugs, were responsible for an abortion, dodged the draft, or cheated on a standardized exam? What makes it worth it?

There may come a time when you feel your child could benefit spiritually from knowing about your past sins or painful experiences. Talking about your past can be a teachable moment with a torpedo-like impact. But how can you make sure that the impact is positive?

Tim Sanford, a licensed professional counselor, offers these general guidelines on presenting potentially harmful information to your older children or teens:

1. Deal with your past sins or traumatic experiences before discussing them with your child. You must be at spiritual and emotional peace before talking with your teen or older child.

2. What you say, and when you say it, must always be for your child's benefit, not your benefit. Do not do this to relieve your anxiety, anger, need to vent, desire to get back at your ex-spouse or cleanse your conscience.

3. Always tell the truth; never lie. You may decline to say something or withhold graphic information, but don't whitewash the events. If children catch you in one lie, they will wonder what else you've been lying about.

4. If the details are unsavory, give only enough of them to get your desired point across. If your children press you for more information, simply decline by saying something like "The details aren't the point here; what is important is that by making bad choices, I put myself and others at risk."

5. Teens usually are mature enough to handle the information and would prefer to hear it from you, not indirectly. If you fear that at the upcoming reunion Aunt Sophie is going to tell your sons or daughters about your "partying days," better they hear it first from you. The added benefit is that you're on the offensive against sin, not defending your reputation.

6. Talk with them when you have time to talk it through completely. Don't rush the time or "just slip it in" somewhere. If you're caught off guard by a question, give yourself time to think what the wisest answer is. You may even want to ask your spouse for support or guidance and pray before broaching the subject. That's fine; tell your child something like "That's a good question, and you deserve the best answer I can give. I need to think about it first."

7. Give them the chance to ask questions, and be as honest as you can if and when they do ask.

8. Share with them the journey from "mistake" to "healing" as well. They need to see and hear more than just the outline of the account and the happily-ever-after ending; they need to understand God's grace through the process.

Evaluate the emotional, social, and spiritual maturity of your child before talking about mistakes you've made. Sensitive issues should be shared one-on-one, perhaps when you are on a trip alone together. It takes time for children to digest such information, and you want to be there and focused on them while they are processing the painful or disappointing news. Along with the consequences of the mistake, you need to teach that knowledge has responsibility.

If there is a chance your children will use the information as an excuse to say, "Mom (or Dad) did it, and she turned out okay," wait, or point out clearly that "okay" is not what God wants for them. God wants the best.

—Jim Weidmann and Marianne Hering[10]

Chapter 6

PRACTICAL TIPS

Make the most of the time you're already with your children. That will go a long way toward helping them understand how God's truth is relevant to their daily lives.

As you do all this, don't expect perfection. Keep cool if you're interrupted, or if funny things happen.

That's what Joe and his wife have to do. They often read from the Book of Proverbs with their two sons, sometimes while they're riding to school in the car. One day, Joe's second-grade son was reading in Proverbs 5. Things were going great until he got to verses 18 and 19:

> May your fountain be blessed,
> and may you rejoice in the wife of your youth.
> A loving doe, a graceful deer—
> may her *beasts* satisfy you always,
> may you ever be captivated by her love. (italics added)

Now, that word isn't really "beasts." The boy missed an "R" in there somewhere. But Joe and his wife didn't think that was the best time to correct him and answer all the questions that would surely follow. For the moment, they had to just suppress their laughter and keep going.

Despite occasional glitches like that, Proverbs is a great book for families to read together. . . . You might want to read ahead a little, though, so you're ready for what your children may find!

We have such limited time with our kids. But God will bring teachable moments our way. Look for those openings and use them to point to God's glory and His plan for the lives of your children.

—Carey Casey
CEO, National Center for Fathering[11]

Identifying Your Needs

Take a couple of minutes to fill out the following survey.

1. Your number-one spiritual training goal for the next year is
   ____ to inspire your child to become an on-fire follower of Jesus.
   ____ to fan the feeble flame of faith in your child's heart.
   ____ to keep yourself from spontaneously combusting.
   ____ other _____

2. You'll know your child is a true disciple when he
   ____ asks himself, "What would Jesus do?"
   ____ grows a beard and wears sandals.
   ____ sends e-mails in King James English.
   ____ other _____

3. The best "teachable moments" you've had with your child were
   ____ at bedtime and at meal times.
   ____ in the car and in the kitchen.
   ____ under protest and under duress.
   ____ other _____

4. Your child's idea of a great "family night" is
    ____ a two-hour devotional on the subject of tithing.
    ____ pizza and air hockey.
    ____ being as far away from you as possible.
    ____ other _____

5. The service project you most wish your child would undertake is
    ____ building an orphanage in Guatemala.
    ____ visiting a nursing home.
    ____ picking the crushed Doritos out of the carpet in his room.
    ____ other _____

6. Signing a family covenant committing yourself to spiritual training
    ____ sounds like a good idea.
    ____ makes you tired just thinking about it.
    ____ is your top priority, right after memorizing the genealogy
    in Matthew 1
    ____ other _____

Watching and Discussing the DVD

Author Mark Holmen thinks most of us need a "makeover" to bring Christ and Christlike living back into our homes. That's where the most effective spiritual training can take place.

But makeovers don't happen without a step-by-step plan. When it comes to raising real believers, that starts with a family mission statement. It's the place to name the values you most want to pass along to your kids.

Then comes a family covenant, your strategy for fulfilling your mission. It gets specific, naming action steps for the next week, month, and year.

Writing a mission statement and covenant—and signing it—can be one of the most practical, rewarding parts of your family's spiritual journey. Are you ready to give it a try?

After viewing the DVD, use questions like these to help you think through what you saw and heard.

1. Mark Holmen believes it's important to have prayer, Bible reading, devotions, family worship, and conversations about faith in our homes. What's your reaction?
   - "Nobody does that stuff anymore."
   - "At least I feel guilty for not doing it. Does that count?"
   - "Who has time for all that?"
   - "It works for my family already."
   - other _____

2. For Mark and his wife, a long driving trip was the catalyst to create a family mission statement. Which of the following would be a catalyst for you?
   - discovering that your child thinks Noah's ark is part of an Indiana Jones movie
   - discovering that your child has stopped believing in miracles
   - discovering that your child will graduate from high school in three days
   - other _____

3. What seemed to be your family's "mission" when you were growing up? Was it intentional or accidental? Was spiritual growth a part of it? What would you say was your family's most cherished value? Why?

4. When it comes to writing a family mission statement and covenant, which of the following do you think your family members would be

most likely to agree on? To disagree on? How might you handle those disagreements?
  • your family's nonnegotiable values
  • goals for spiritual growth
  • action steps
  • grammar and punctuation

5. Which of the following would you most want your family mission statement to resemble? Why?
  • the Declaration of Independence
  • the *Star Trek* Prime Directive
  • the Ten Commandments
  • the Lord's Prayer
  • the Pledge of Allegiance
  • other _____

6. Which of the following documents would you most want your family covenant to resemble? Why?
  • the U.S. Constitution
  • the owner's manual for your car
  • the End User License Agreement for Microsoft Office
  • the Canadian national anthem
  • the Book of Leviticus
  • other _____

7. Which of the following roles would your child, if he or she is old enough, be most interested in? If you have more than one child, specify the role each one might like. How could your answer to this question make creating a family mission statement and covenant easier?
  • reminding everyone of action steps
  • celebrating completion of action steps

- making a list of values
- polishing the phrasing of your mission

8. How could having a family mission statement and covenant help you in the following situations?
    - Your kids fidget during family prayer and Bible reading.
    - You've overextended yourself in volunteering for jobs at church.
    - Your daughter wants to sponsor an orphan, but your other kids don't care.
    - You fear you've waited too long to do anything about spiritual training.

Bible Study

As iron sharpens iron,
so one man sharpens another. (Proverbs 27:17)

1. Has interacting with a mentor or friend ever "sharpened" your commitment as a follower of Jesus? If so, how?

   If you've tried to train your child spiritually, have you and he sharpened each other or just rubbed each other the wrong way? Explain.

   Carry each other's burdens, and in this way you will fulfill the law of Christ. (Galatians 6:2)

2. Which of the following might be slowing down your child's spiritual growth?

___ a chore or job that keeps him from spending time in the Bible or with other Christians

___ an emotional weight (guilt, low self-esteem) that discourages him from approaching God or trying new things

___ stress that steals his energy and preoccupies his thoughts

How could you help carry that burden?

> *Therefore confess your sins to each other and pray for each other so that you may be healed. The prayer of a righteous man is powerful and effective. (James 5:16)*

3. Have you ever confessed a sin to your child? If so, what happened? If not, why not?

Have you ever asked your child to pray for you? If so, what happened? If not, why not?

> *I am not writing this to shame you, but to warn you, as my dear children. Even though you have ten thousand guardians in Christ, you do not have many fathers, for in Christ Jesus I became your father through the gospel. Therefore I urge you to imitate me.*
> *. . . Follow my example, as I follow the example of Christ. (1 Corinthians 4:14-16; 11:1)*

4. Would you feel comfortable making statements like these to your child? Why or why not?

What's one way in which you're trying to follow Christ's example?

Has your child seen you doing that? If so, what happened? If not, why not?

Applying the Principles

Want to start your "family makeover"? Writing a family mission statement is a great place to begin. Here's the mission statement Mark Holmen's family came up with:

HOLMEN FAMILY MISSION STATEMENT

"The Holmen family is a Christian family who unconditionally loves, supports, nurtures, and forgives each other, who demonstrates fiscal responsibility, including giving of our time, talents, and treasure to the Lord, and who models faith in Christlike living through what we think, say, and do."

Now it's your turn. The process will take awhile, but you can start this way:

1. Make a list of values that are nonnegotiable—absolute—to members of your family. Let all family members who are old enough to participate do so.
2. Share these values with each other and choose the ones you want to appear in your mission statement.
3. Put the values in sentence form.

Then ask yourselves:

- Is this mission statement specific enough to hold you accountable as a family?
- Is it likely to stand the test of time?
- What would Jesus think of it?

Once you've come up with a mission statement, your next step will be to write a family covenant—your strategy for fulfilling your mission statement. This should include action steps for the week, month, and year. Negotiate your covenant as a family until all of you are ready to sign it.

To begin, look at the following list. Circle four values that are important to you. Then add four others that aren't on the list. Ask your family to do the same this week.

UNCONDITIONAL LOVE	GRACE
SUPPORT	LEARNING GOD'S WORD
NURTURE	PROTECTING THE ENVIRONMENT
FORGIVENESS	DEFENDING LIFE
FISCAL RESPONSIBILITY	PHYSICAL EXERCISE
GIVING	CREATIVITY
CHRISTLIKE LIVING	MUSIC
FUN	GOOD NUTRITION
SHARING FAITH	EDUCATION
SEEKING JUSTICE	HELPING NEIGHBORS
TRADITION	PRAYING FOR OTHERS
MISSIONS	POLITICS
HUMOR	SPORTS
TECHNOLOGY	TRAVEL
PURITY	USING SPIRITUAL GIFTS
WORSHIP	PEACE
_____	_____
_____	_____

Insight for Your Week

Sometimes asking your kids questions is better than giving them answers.

"Jesus died on the cross like Frogger died in the water?" Justin, almost four, asked. He was trying to make sense of a video game where the main character, a frog, has five lives each session.

"Yes," I (Marianne) said hesitantly.

"Don't worry," he said. "Jesus will come back just like Frogger."

"Is Frogger real?" I asked.

"Yes."

"Is Jesus real?" I asked.

"Yes."

I then tried to explain the difference between Jesus, whom Justin has never seen, and the very visual Frogger, whom he sees too much of.

By asking our kids questions, we can find out about them and what they need to know. Using questions instead of lectures to teach our children accomplishes three things:

1. It builds the relationship.

2. It starts a conversation.

3. It keeps the information specific to what your kids need to know at that precise moment.

If you want to start a conversation with your kids, here are some sample questions on the topic of friendship. (The questions are geared for middle school kids on up. For younger children, rephrase the questions in a way they can understand.)

- Which student/friend is the kindest in your class or group of friends? What does he or she do that you like? Why do you want to be that person's friend?

- Who is the least popular kid at school? What does that kid feel like when he or she is at school?

- How do you treat that kid? How would Jesus treat that kid?

- If something really embarrassing happened to you, which one of your friends would be least likely to tell your secret? How do you know?

- If you all went to the mall together, which one of your friends might ask you to shoplift? Which one would be most likely to say, "That's wrong"?

- Who is the person at school least likely to get in a fight? Why did you choose that person? Would you like to be more like that person?
- Who are the Christians in your class? How can you tell?
- Where do you eat lunch? Who sits with you?
- Who are the three most important people to you? Did you talk to them today? What about?
- Who is the most unhappy person in your class or among your friends? How do you know? What can you do for that person?
- Which one of your friends will give you the best advice? Why did you choose that person? Would the advice be based on the Bible? If not, what would it be based on?
- What are your standards for choosing friends? Which of your friends comes closest to that standard? Which one is farthest from that standard?
- Do you want more friends? Why?
- What does it feel like when a friend lets you down? Will Jesus ever let you down?

—Jim Weidmann and Marianne Hering[12]

NOTES

1. Carey Casey with Neil Wilson, *Championship Fathering* (Carol Stream, Ill.: Focus on the Family/Tyndale House Publishers, 2009), pp. 135-136.
2. Adapted from Jim Weidmann and Marianne Hering, *The Power of Teachable Moments* (Carol Stream, Ill.: Focus on the Family/Tyndale House Publishers, 2004), pp. 6-9.
3. Casey and Wilson, pp. 103-104.
4. Weidmann and Hering, pp. 83-86.
5. Casey and Wilson, pp. 42-43.
6. Weidmann and Hering, pp. 13-15.
7. Casey and Wilson, pp. 97-98.
8. Weidmann and Hering, pp. 105-107.
9. Casey and Wilson, pp. 122-123.
10. Weidmann and Hering, pp. 155-159.
11. Casey and Wilson, pp. 148-149.
12. Weidmann and Hering, pp. 64-68.

About Our DVD Presenters

Essentials of Parenting:
Raising Kids with a Faith that Lasts

Dr. Tim Kimmel is the executive director of Family Matters® and has spoken throughout the country at Family Matters' Raising Truly Great Kids conferences; Promise Keepers; Focus on the Family's Life on the Edge tour; and with his wife, Darcy, at FamilyLife Ministry's Weekend to Remember conferences. His books include *Grace-Based Parenting, Raising Kids for True Greatness, Why Christian Kids Rebel,* and *Little House on the Freeway.* He and Darcy also authored *Extreme Grandparenting.*

Rev. Mark Holmen is the author of *Faith Begins at Home* and *Building Faith at Home.* He served as the senior pastor of Ventura Missionary Church in California for over eight years, where he developed and implemented the internationally known Faith at Home movement.

Larry Fowler has served the Awana ministry as club director, missionary, curriculum writer, program developer, author, conference speaker, seminar leader, youth pastor, doctrinal expert, Bible teacher, executive director of international ministries, in the U.S. program and training, and currently global training and the Rorheim Institute. He is the author of *Rock-Solid Kids* and *Raising a Modern-Day Joseph.* Larry and his wife, Diane, have two children and seven grandchildren.

ESSENTIALS OF PARENTING™

Resources from Focus on the Family®

In *Essentials of Parenting™: Raising Kids with a Faith that Lasts*, authorities like Dr. Tim Kimmel, Mark Holmen, and Larry Fowler introduce you to one of your greatest privileges—helping your child begin a relationship with God. Includes a six-session DVD and a Resource CD-ROM with Leader's Guide, Participant's Guide, Campaign Planning Guide, and print-ready promotional materials.*

In *Essentials of Parenting™: The Power of Love*, experts like Carey Casey, Gary Thomas, and Dr. Juli Slattery show how to enrich and enjoy the bond between your child and yourself. Includes a six-session DVD and a Resource CD-ROM with Leader's Guide, Participant's Guide, Campaign Planning Guide, and print-ready promotional materials.*

In *Essentials of Parenting™: Be Prepared*, mentors like Dannah Gresh, Dr. Bob Barnes, and Dr. Juli Slattery present practical plans for dealing with dangers, including Internet porn, alcohol, drugs, eating disorders, and premarital sex. Includes a seven-session DVD and a Resource CD-ROM with Leader's Guide, Participant's Guide, Campaign Planning Guide, and print-ready promotional materials.*

*Printed Participant's Guides also available for purchase at FocusOnTheFamily.com/resources

FocusOnTheFamily.com

For more information log on to FocusOnTheFamily.com/Resources or call toll-free: 800-A-FAMILY

In Canada, log on to FocusOnTheFamily.ca or call toll-free: 800-661-9800

CP0426